GIRL ASLEEP

Matthew Whittet

Currency Press, Sydney

BELVOIR

CURRENT THEATRE SERIES

First published in 2016
by Currency Press Pty Ltd,
PO Box 2287, Strawberry Hills, NSW, 2012, Australia
enquiries@currency.com.au
www.currency.com.au

in association with Belvoir, Sydney

Cataloguing-in-publication data for this title is available from the National
Library of Australia website: www.nla.gov.au

Typeset by Dean Nottle for Currency Press.
Cover image: Amber McMahon by Brett Boardman.
Cover design by Alphabet Studio.

Currency Press acknowledges the Traditional Owners of the Country on which
we live and work. We pay our respects to all Aboriginal and Torres Strait
Islander Elders, past and present.

Contents

Girl Asleep was first produced by Windmill Performing Arts at The Space, Adelaide, as part of Adelaide Festival on 28 February 2014, with the following cast:

LITTLE GRETA	Zara Blight
ELLIOTT / SERGE GAINSBOURG	Eamon Farren
GENEVIEVE / FIREBIRD / JADE	Jude Henshall
JANET / QUEEN / UMBER / DENISE MACKEL	Amber McMahon
GRETA	Ellen Steele
LITTLE GRETA	Paige Whitby
CONRAD / GOBLIN	Matthew Whittet

Director, Rosemary Myers
Designer, Jonathon Oxlade
Lighting Designer, Richard Vabre
Composer, Luke Smiles (motion laboratories)
Animation, Chris More

CHARACTERS

GRETA

GENEVIEVE

JANET

CONRAD

ELLIOTT

JADE

UMBER

FINN GRETA

SERGE GAINSBOURG

CRONE

LITTLE GRETA

FIREBIRD

QUEEN

GOBLIN

DENISE MACKEL

GUESTS

SETTING

Somewhere in suburbia. 1970's.

This play went to press before the end of rehearsals and may differ from the play as performed.

In dialogue, a forward slash (/) is used to indicate interrupted or overlapping speech.

A teenage girl is in her bedroom. She is dressed in her best seventies party frock. It's like she's sleepwalking. Her hair covers her face and her movement is dreamy.

GRETA: Don't ask me to explain what happened that night. All I know is the facts. The ones that I saw, the ones I thought I saw, and the ones I know in my heart to be true. It was my fifteenth birthday. My parents decided to throw me a party, even though it was the last thing I wanted. But during the night, something happened. Something strange. And nothing would ever be the same again.

> GRETA *starts to fall. She falls in slow motion, like she is dropping from an immense height. The sound of wind rushes all around her as she seems to gather immense speed, but she still moves in slow motion.*

> *It seems as if she is about to meet the cold, hard ground beneath her, when everything suddenly goes black.*

But first, let's go back.

> *A photo of* GRETA *appears on the wall. She's an eight-year-old with a huge goofy smile, holding a music box.*

This is me when I was eight. Apparently I was so noisy and fearless back then. Nothing would stop me. I was like the completely crazy one in the family.

> *We see* CONRAD, *her dad. He's a vision of 1970's beige.*

This is my dad. His name's Conrad.

CONRAD: Where's my little princess?

GRETA: And even though he tells the worst jokes ever …

CONRAD: Hey, have you seen that new movie? What's it called …? Ah. *Constipation.*

> *He waits for an answer.*

GRETA: I've still got a soft spot for them. I may actually be the last person on earth who still finds them funny.

CONRAD: You haven't? That's because it hasn't come out yet. You saw *Diarrhoea* though? It got leaked early.

We see her mum. JANET *looks like she was beautiful once, but not anymore. She's hardened by life, holding a gin and tonic and looking depressed.*

GRETA: This is my mum. Janet. When she was a teenager she was incredibly beautiful. She still is, if you ask me. She competed in twenty-six different pageants by the time she was nineteen, and won practically all of them. My dad was her biggest fan. But when she turned twenty, everything came to a screeching halt. My sister came along.

A song by French crooner Serge Gainsbourg plays on a record player in another room.

JANET: *Genevieve?!*

An older girl, GENEVIEVE, *appears, dressed like Jean Seberg in* Breathless. *She always looks like she will punch you if you dared speak to her.*

GENEVIEVE: *What?!*

GRETA: My older sister. Genevieve.

JANET: Can you turn that Serge Gainsbourg rubbish down please!

CONRAD: We like things a little French, but that's getting a bit too continental for our liking.

GENEVIEVE *glares at him with a stare that would turn milk sour.*

GRETA: She's obsessed with Serge Gainsbourg. I'm pretty sure it's mainly because Mum hates him so much.

GENEVIEVE *gives them a death stare and reluctantly turns the music off.*

She dropped out of school two months ago and has a part-time job selling cosmetics door to door, but as soon as she saves enough money she'll be on the first plane out of here. Bound for Paris.

CONRAD: Are you staying home for dinner, Genevieve? A family meal at least one night this week would be nice.

GENEVIEVE: It depends. Will I have to look at your face while I do it, Conrad?

JANET: His name is Dad! Show your father some respect!

GENEVIEVE: What, like you do, Janet?

JANET *sucks in her breath. Appalled.* CONRAD *disappears.*

JANET: You're treading on thin ice, Genevieve! Thin ice!

Fadeout.

GRETA: So that's my family. I love them, but sometimes it's hard to stay on the roller-coaster, if you know what I mean.

The lights come up slowly on GRETA, *standing in her school uniform.*

We move around heaps 'cause of my dad's work, so I'm always starting at new schools. I'm up to my fourth in the last year alone. And I hate it. I totally and utterly hate it.

An awkward, gangly young guy wanders in, yelling out to another boy offstage. This is ELLIOTT.

ELLIOTT: Whatever, Steven! At least I've got manners!

He sees GRETA *and sidles up to her.*

Greta. That's a good name. What's it short for? Gretel? Margareta?

She shakes her head.

Or just Greta? You know, as in Greta short for … Greta?

She nods.

Right. Cool. Are you fourteen?

She nods.

Snap! Me too, hey. Fourteen is good, huh, but I'm seriously looking forward to fifteen. I think fifteen is going to turn a corner. It's going to be awesome. It's going to herald the dawn of a new era, or something like that. Are you from around here?

She shakes her head.

That's fine if you're not, you know, 'cause I am. From around here. I know pretty much everything there is to know about around here. Population, elevation, average rainfall, climate, local industries, that sort of thing. Have you got any brothers?

She shakes her head.

Oh, okay. What about sisters?

GRETA: Yeah.

ELLIOTT: Awesome! Sisters are the best. What about friends? 'Cause we can be friends if you want. I'm pretty non-judgemental. I'm usually happy to just go with the flow actually, I find that's the best way to be friendly with people. I've got six guinea pigs. I count them as good friends. But their life span tends to hamper things a little. So what do you reckon? Should we just hang or something? We don't have to. I haven't got much else to do so … I don't mind really. It's up to you. Whatever. I'm easy. It could be nice. But no pressure.

    GRETA *speaks really softly.*

GRETA: … Sure.

ELLIOTT: Really? Oh, awesome! Good choice. I like your thinking.

    They hang for a moment.

This is good. I actually love this. I love this a lot. New friends, new perspectives. It's such a tonic. It really is.

GRETA: I guess.

ELLIOTT: We should get a donut! We should celebrate this with a donut.

GRETA: … Umm … okay …

ELLIOTT: Wait here. Just … wait here.

    ELLIOTT *runs off.*

    Two girls approach GRETA *from the other direction. Twins,* JADE *and* UMBER. *They stare at her for some time in silence. Like they are undressing her with their eyes. They are terrifying. Eventually one of them speaks.*

JADE: Umber wants to know what you think of my hair? I don't like it anymore, but she thinks it frames my cheekbones in a way that bangs like yours wouldn't.

    She looks at UMBER, *who just stares straight at* JADE, *like they are having a silent conversation.* JADE *laughs suddenly.*

I know what you mean, but why wouldn't anyone else want that with a Kahlua and Coke?

    UMBER *stares at* GRETA. GRETA *has no idea what's going on.*

    ELLIOTT *runs in with two strawberry donuts, but stops dead in his tracks when he sees the twins.*

ELLIOTT: *Hey, Greta!*

    They both look at him in utter disgust.

    UMBER *looks back at* GRETA, *then walks off.* JADE *looks back to* GRETA.

JADE: So, it's agreed. We'll see you at three-thirty outside the servo. She's taken quite a shine to you.

GRETA: Umm, I'm not sure if I can … /

JADE: Shhh shh sh.

She stares intensely at GRETA *for a moment.*

I like you, quiet girl. Don't spoil it now by speaking. You're new, and we're giving you a chance. Three-thirty. [*Indicating* ELLIOTT] He's not invited.

JADE *leaves.*

ELLIOTT *goes to leave with his donuts.*

ELLIOTT: Wow. Jade and Umber, huh? Well, good luck with your new friends then.

ELLIOTT *goes to leave, but* GRETA *stops him.*

GRETA: Please, don't let them be my friends.

His jaw drops.

ELLIOTT: You're not going to meet them this arvo?

She shakes her head.

GRETA: They're terrifying.

ELLIOTT: So you're not gonna be friends with them? You sure about that?

GRETA *nods.*

Alright.

They both hang out in silence together.

ELLIOTT *offers her a donut. She takes it from him and they both quietly munch away.* ELLIOTT *smiles at her.*

Good donut. Donuts are the best! Don't you think?

GRETA *smiles and nods her head.*

Awesome. Awesome donuts.

GRETA *thinks for a moment.*

GRETA: Should we go hang out at my place this arvo?

ELLIOTT: I'm easy. Whatever. I'm cool. Yes. I'd like that. That would be lovely, thank you.

Blackout.

GRETA: My room is my haven. My little bubble that protects me from the outside world. Normally it would take me ages to invite a friend over to see it, but then again normally it would take me ages to find a friend, full stop.

♦ ♦ ♦ ♦ ♦ ♦ ♦ ♦ ♦ ♦

Lights come up on GRETA *and* ELLIOTT *in her bedroom. It glows and hums. They both sit on the floor and* GRETA *instantly starts to relax.*

GRETA: Pretty cool, huh.

ELLIOTT: You've got plastic horses! I can't believe it! I love plastic horses.

GRETA: Some of this stuff … I've had forever. Since I was a little girl. Every time we move somewhere new, I unpack all this, and I instantly feel better.

ELLIOTT: I have plastic pigs at home. I collect plastic pigs.

GRETA: Do you like my paper cranes? They're made out of letters from my penpal in Finland.

ELLIOTT: Finland?! Oh, my God, that is so freaking exotic!

GRETA: Her name's Greta too. We love calling each other Greta.

They both put on silly high-pitched voices.

ELLIOTT: *Oh, hello there, Greta!*

GRETA: *Oh yes, hi, Greta.*

ELLIOTT: *How are you today, Greta?*

GRETA: *Good thank you, Greta.*

I'll read you one.

GRETA *takes one of the cranes down, unfolding it gently.*

ELLIOTT: How do you do that? Those folds are so freaking little.

GRETA: [*reading*] 'Dearest Greta. How are you in the land of the sunshine, Greta? Better, Greta, than freezing in the winter of the Helsinki, Greta, where the sun is shining never, Greta.'

ELLIOTT: Oh, my God, she is awesome.

GRETA: I know.

ELLIOTT: Keep going, keep going!

GRETA: [*reading*] 'How is the new town you are living in, Greta? I hope the kindness of the other children is happening this time … I must finish. Today is national costume day at my school so I must go wear my *kansallispuvu*. That is the name of the national costume. 'Bye 'bye, Greta. Love you heaps, Greta.'

ELLIOTT: Wow. You should go like on exchange to Finland or something and meet her. How cold would that be!

GRETA: I know. It'd be amazing.

He sees a picture on the wall. A large, framed photo of a young girl dressed up nicely, holding a music box.

ELLIOTT: Holy crap balls! Is that you?

GRETA *blushes.*

GRETA: Yeah …

ELLIOTT: It's so cute!

GRETA: It's me when I was eight. My dad loves that picture so much. See what I'm holding?

ELLIOTT: Yeah.

GRETA: Listen.

She goes to her windowsill and picks up the same music box that's in the picture. She opens it with a key that's on a chain around her neck.

Beautiful light and music emerge from it. Like a gentle bedtime tune from another world. A fairytale world.

My mum gave it to me on my eighth birthday.

ELLIOTT: Whoa.

GRETA: Be careful. It's really old. You might get a splinter. It used to be hers when she was a kid. I used to imagine that it was made by a magician in a faraway realm.

ELLIOTT: Whoa … a magician.

GRETA: Yeah, from a realm where like almost anything could happen. One that's filled with incredible, mystical creatures and castles stuffed with untold treasures.

ELLIOTT: Whoa … that sounds like the Vatican.

GRETA: And that the magic inside this piece of music kept the entire realm safe from the dangers that lurked beyond its borders. Hidden in the shadows. It's the most beautiful thing ever.

She stares silently into the box for a moment, the song casting a spell.

While she is lost in the spell of the song, we see the curtains in her window billow gently, like a wind has just kissed them from a distant land.

GRETA *snaps the box shut—the spell gone in an instant.*

But that was a long time ago. I was just a little kid back then.

ELLIOTT: Music is so good, don't you think?!

GRETA *puts her box safely away, back up on the shelf.*

They both fall into an easy silence together.

It's easy with you, Greta. Who needs any of those other idiots in our year? 'Oh, you're so short … and tall!' All anyone needs is one good friend. I'm glad you're my friend.

GRETA: Yeah, me too, Elliott. Me too.

ELLIOTT: Good friends.

GRETA: Great friends.

ELLIOTT: Yeah. My sentiment exactly.

Lights slowly fade on this image of peace and tranquillity.

GRETA: This here, this is my life. My family, my friend, people at school … I kinda thought I had it all in check. Until about a week ago.

GRETA *joins* JANET *and* GENEVIEVE *at the breakfast table.*

My mum announced at breakfast …

JANET: It's your birthday next week, darling. Your father and I thought we'd throw you a little party to celebrate.

GRETA *prickles at this news.*

GRETA: What? When was this decided?

JANET: It's just a little celebratory get-together. That's all.

GRETA: But I don't want a party!

GENEVIEVE: Oh, my God, Greta, just be grateful, will you? I was never offered anything like that when I was your age. All I got was, 'Which Pizza Hut do you want to go to this year?'

JANET: And what's wrong with Pizza Hut? They've got puzzles on the placemats. That's very clever.

CONRAD *comes in.*

CONRAD: What's all the hubbub in here?

GENEVIEVE: Jesus!

CONRAD: Did someone finish off my Special K?

JANET: This is neither the time nor the place for comedy!

GRETA: I'm just saying I don't need a party.

CONRAD: You told her?

GRETA: I'm happy to just go to Pizza Hut again with you guys.

CONRAD: I thought it was supposed to be a surprise!

JANET: [*to* CONRAD] Don't you start! [*To* GRETA] We want to meet more of your friends, that's all. Show off a little. You're a beautiful young woman, but you always hide your light under a bushel. I thought I'd get you a nice dress for the occasion and your sister can do your make-up. We can all do it!

> JANET *sucks in her breath.*

CONRAD: Oh, she doesn't need too much gussying-up, does she? Not my little girl.

GRETA: I'm seriously happy with Pizza Hut. Seriously.

JANET: Some support would be appreciated. It's important for a young girl to have a night where they celebrate with their family and friends. Where they get to emerge as a young woman. Especially when they're turning sweet fifteen.

GENEVIEVE: Sweet sixteen! How can you get everything so wrong?

JANET: Fifteen can be sweet too. [*To* CONRAD] Back me up please.

CONRAD: Let's not get too carried away with this sort of rhetoric, Janet. A party would be nice, but she doesn't need to go down that sort of path, not just yet anyway.

JANET: And what sort of path would that be, Conrad?

CONRAD: Well … there'll be teenage boys here, and … You know what I mean.

GENEVIEVE: If you're not careful you might have two sluts in the family to deal with. Right, Conrad?

CONRAD: Oi, oi oi!

> JANET *is shocked.*

JANET: Genevieve Marie Tippy Driscol! You take that back this instant!

GENEVIEVE: What are you gunna do if I don't, Janet? Revoke my dowry?

CONRAD: You pull your head in, Missy.

GRETA: I'll just do the salad bar if that makes things easier. I won't even have pizza!

JANET: Why is this even happening? [*To* GENEVIEVE] This was a conversation between myself and my daughter about her fifteenth birthday and again you had to bring the mood down. You with your smart mouth and you with your poo-poo ways.

GENEVIEVE: Well, maybe you should have had this conversation with her a week ago, then it all wouldn't have been too late now, would it?!

Beat.

GRETA: What wouldn't have been too late …?

No-one says anything.

JANET: Well … it's just that we've already handed out the invitations.

GENEVIEVE: I told them it was a bad idea.

GRETA: You've handed them out already? To who?

JANET: Just … your teacher. Who passed them around …

GRETA: … To who?

JANET: … Some kids … At school …

GRETA: … How many?

GENEVIEVE *cringes.*

My whole class …?

GENEVIEVE *cringes again.*

My whole year?!

GENEVIEVE *nods reluctantly.*

GRETA *is silent, a strange fury welling up inside her.*

JANET: Conrad?

CONRAD: We just want you to come out of your shell a little more, darling. We think it'll be good for you.

GRETA: You can't do this, you can't do this to me /

CONRAD: Greta /

GRETA: Do you want to destroy my life? I don't want a party!

JANET: I think you're overreacting a little, Pumpkin.

GRETA: Get it through your thick skulls, I don't want a party. *Not here! Not now! Not ever!*

JANET: Greta!

GRETA: *No fucking party! Fuck!*

GENEVIEVE: Whoa … Where'd that come from, Chuck Norris?

They all fall into a shocked silence.

JANET: I take it you don't want a party then.

JANET *is almost in tears, but is keeping herself together.* CONRAD *goes to put his hand on her shoulder, but she flicks him away.*

Fine … I'll cancel everything.

JANET *walks out.* CONRAD *looks at the girls for a moment then follows after her, calling out.*

CONRAD: Janet … Janet!

They both look to where their parents just left. GENEVIEVE *gives* GRETA *a look for a moment, like she's sizing her sister up.*

GENEVIEVE: Well, aren't you the surprise package?

She taps/flicks her on the head, almost cruelly and leaves.

GRETA: I don't know what happened that day. What it was that came out of me. I'd never screamed at anyone like that before. And it scared me.

GRETA *goes to her room, grabs her music box and climbs under her sheets, heading off to bed for the night.*

Later that night when I went to bed I could hear my parents.

From the room next door we can hear CONRAD *and* JANET *start arguing.*

And all I could think was that this was my fault. I let this genie out of the bottle. And I had no idea how to put it back again.

She looks up to her origami cranes.

Greta? I wish you weren't in Finland. I wish you were here.

GRETA *listens to them fighting for a moment.*

They're really going at it hammer and tongs, hurling all sorts of accusations at each other. JANET *is totally ripping him a new one. Like twenty years of frustrations have just been released.* GRETA *sits listening.*

As the fighting escalates from one side, GENEVIEVE *puts on Serge Gainsbourg in her bedroom to drown them out.*

GRETA *is completely stuck in the middle. She can't bear it. She takes her music box out and opens it up. From underneath it all the beautiful song starts to drown everything else out.* GRETA *closes her eyes and loses herself in her favourite piece of music.*

It's like she's managed to retreat into her own bubble now.

She's finally becoming calm again, and drifting off to sleep.

As the last few strains of the music plays, the curtains billow gently again. Just for the tiniest moment we see a pair of old, gnarled hands moving along the window sill from outside, reaching in towards her. The face of the CRONE *appears ...*

Blackout.

♦ ♦ ♦ ♦ ♦ ♦ ♦ ♦ ♦ ♦

GRETA: I thought about it that night. And even though I wanted this party like I wanted a hole in the head, I knew I had no choice. I was going to have to face it, whether I liked it or not.

The lights snap up on an incredibly excited JANET *as she throws her arms around* GRETA.

JANET: Really? Oh, my God! Oh, my God! You won't regret this, darling. You won't regret this one little bit.

She announces to everyone at the top of her lungs.

C'mon, you lazy bones-es. *We've got a party to organise!*

Things shift immediately.

Everyone is running around, setting up for the party.

Happy birthday bunting goes up, platters are being prepared. A kind of set-up montage where JANET, CONRAD *and* GENEVIEVE *run around busying themselves while* GRETA *is in the middle of it all, watching.*

GRETA: The week passed way too quickly, and before I knew it the day itself had arrived. And all I wanted to do was vomit. Continuously. In my own mouth. Vomit!

JANET *calls out to* CONRAD.

JANET: Genevieve? I need help with the decorations! They're not going to hang themselves, now are they?!

GENEVIEVE: I'm making a playlist, Janet! Do you want me to help or not?

JANET: None of that Serge Gainsbourg rubbish please.

GENEVIEVE: It'll be what I say it'll be!

JANET: It's way too sexualised for my liking, thank you very much.

GENEVIEVE: What's wrong with a bit of sexy?

CONRAD: You used to like it all a bit sexy, didn't you, Janet?

GENEVIEVE: Oh, God. Here we go.

> JANET *puts her fingers in her ears and sings, blocking out what* CONRAD *is saying.*

CONRAD: Those were the days. Weren't they, Janet? Weren't they? When you found things sexy. Remember? Back in the good old days?

GENEVIEVE: Keep digging, Conrad.

JANET: Get out! Go make yourself useful. We need ice for the punch. Go!

CONRAD: Sorry, what was that?

JANET: Ice.

CONRAD: Yeah … ice …

> *A horrible, awkward moment passes between* JANET *and* CONRAD. *He goes.*

JANET: Right. We better get cracking. Are you ready, darling?

GRETA: Please, Mum … I don't want to go to too much trouble. I just thought I'd keep it casual … Like Dad said, I don't need too much gussying-up. Maybe I could just wear my overalls …?

GENEVIEVE: No chance, Greta. Janet's been shopping.

JANET: We better get to work. There's not much time.

> *They turn to* GRETA *and start to approach her.*

GRETA: Oh, God … please … I don't want this … *I don't want this at all!*

> JANET *and* GENEVIEVE *pounce on her and set to work. Much flurrying of fabrics and make-up and such.*
>
> *Eventually she's revealed.*
>
> *She looks incredible.*
>
> *She's totally transformed, from an innocent teen with her hair pulled back, to a vision of 1970's feminine beauty. A long, flowing dress with wedges and her hair straight and long down her back.*
>
> *They both stare at her in complete shock. They can't believe that this is the same girl.* GRETA *looks at them both, fearful of their response.*

… What? … What is it?

> *They don't say anything.*

Tell me! I look horrible, don't I?

GENEVIEVE *runs off.*

JANET *gets a little emotional.*

GENEVIEVE *runs back in with a mirror.*

GENEVIEVE: See for yourself.

GRETA *looks in the mirror.*

She's taken aback as well. But more in a way where she's not sure if she even recognises herself.

GRETA *can't speak. She's in shock.*

JANET: You look beautiful. So grown-up …

GRETA *still can't speak.*

Pause.

An alarm goes off in the kitchen.

That'll be my baby quiches.

JANET *goes from the room, leaving* GENEVIEVE *holding the mirror up to* GRETA.

GENEVIEVE *looks at her for a moment.*

GENEVIEVE: You remember my fifteenth?

GRETA *nods.*

Be careful. Crazy shit can happen.

JANET *can be heard in the kitchen.*

JANET: [*off*] Oh, they're perfect. They're just perfect.
GRETA: What?
GENEVIEVE: Craaaazy shit.
GRETA: What the hell are you talking about?
GENEVIEVE: I'll be watching. Like a hawk.

JANET *comes into the room with oven mitts on and carrying a tray with baby quiches. She's bustling through the room and out the other side.*

JANET: Ladies, we're on a schedule. People will be arriving before you can say, 'Oh, hello, don't you look lovely'.
GENEVIEVE: Jesus, Janet! Keep it in your liners, will you?!

The front door bell rings.

JANET: Oh no, this is a disaster. Someone's arrived early. I'm not ready at all.

GENEVIEVE: I'll get it!

She opens the door. ELLIOTT *walks in. He is dressed in a suit. Maybe something velvet with frills.*

It's not anyone important. It's just Elliott.

ELLIOTT: Thanks.

GENEVIEVE: Whatever.

ELLIOTT: No, really. Thanks. I would never have gotten in the door if you hadn't opened it.

GENEVIEVE: You're weird.

ELLIOTT: No.

GRETA *slowly comes in. They both stand staring at each other for a long moment. Neither really knows what to say.* ELLIOTT *is stunned, and* GRETA *is still in a state of shock from earlier.*

Wow … you …

GRETA: Don't say another word or I will punch you in the fucken balls.

Silence.

ELLIOTT *mouths the word 'okay'.*

None of this was my idea. They made me do this. They've painted me up like a stupid doll. I don't even like wearing dresses.

ELLIOTT *mouths silently again, 'You look amazing. I didn't even recognise you. I mean I did recognise you, but you just look so … different. Good different.'*

GRETA *sighs.*

You can speak, you know.

ELLIOTT: But you said you were going to punch me in the balls.

GRETA: I'm not going to … You don't have to be so literal, Elliott.

ELLIOTT: Good. 'Cause I value my texticles.

GRETA: I just feel … set upon, you know?

ELLIOTT: Yeah. Sure.

GRETA: I told them I didn't want a party. I didn't want people who I hardly know here. They'll take one look at me and think I'm a complete deadshit moron.

ELLIOTT: Who cares what anyone else thinks?

GRETA: They will! Just look at me.

ELLIOTT: Hey, what do you think of my suit?

GRETA: It's nice. I'd much rather wear that than this.

ELLIOTT: Really?

GRETA: I hate dresses. That suit looks great. It makes you look good.

ELLIOTT: Seriously?

GRETA: Yeah, totally. You might even get lucky tonight.

> ELLIOTT *looks surprised for a moment.*

ELLIOTT: … With who?

GRETA: I hear Denise Mackel might be coming. She's got her eye on you, you know.

ELLIOTT: Which one? Denise Mackel's got crazy eyes. I can never even tell what she's looking at.

> *The front door bell starts to ring.*

> JANET *calls from off.*

JANET: [*off*] Guests are arriving! Let them in, Greta! Let them in, for Christ's sake!

ELLIOTT: … Denise Mackel? … Really?

> *Pause.*

> Greta … there's something I've been meaning to tell you /

JANET: [*off*] Elliott, get in here and help me with these vol-au-vents.

> *Awkward pause.*

> *The front door bell rings again.*

GRETA: Umm. I better get that. Tell me later? Okay?

ELLIOTT: [*calling to* JANET] Are you using anchovy paste, Janet?! You have to use anchovy paste if you're to get that right kind of salty!

> ELLIOTT *runs off.*

> GRETA *looks to where he went for a moment. Wondering what he was going to tell her.*

> *The bell pulls her attention back to the door again.*

GENEVIEVE: Answer the door, idiot.

> GRETA *looks at herself in the mirror.*

GRETA: You can do this, Greta.

> *The front door bell rings again, but this time it's twice as loud and much more insistent.* GRETA *jumps.*

> *She takes a deep breath and heads towards the door. The bell is ringing like crazy now, getting louder and louder. It's almost unbearable. Crowds of kids can be heard on the other side of the door.*

The world isn't going to end. The sky isn't going to fall in. You can do this.

> GRETA *braces herself and opens the door.*

> *Blackout.*

> *There's very loud party music playing.*

◆ ◆ ◆ ◆ ◆ ◆ ◆ ◆ ◆

The party.

GRETA *is in the hallway. A steady stream of people come through with presents. She is handed something from everyone who goes past.*

A whole procession dances through.

DENISE MACKEL *runs up to her.*

DENISE: *Hi, Greta. Great party! Where's the party?! Inside there?!*

> *She is incredibly loud and has a lazy eye.*

> *Here's a present! My mum said I had to get you a present! It's a cat! There's a cat in that box!*

GRETA: Hey! Denise Mackel, right?

DENISE: *Yeah, totally! We're in Science together, dumbo head! Have you seen Elliott?! Elliott's dreamy! Where is he?!*

GRETA: He's down the hall.

DENISE: *Really?! I'm gunna try get me a piece of him later! Wish me luck!*

> ELLIOTT *walks in and* DENISE *sees him. He stops dead in his tracks, like a deer in headlights.*

> *Oh, my God, Elliott! There you are, Elliott! I'm going to put you in a headlock!*

ELLIOTT: Greta. Help me. Please.

DENISE: *I'm going to do rasperries on your belly! Come here, dreamboat!*

She runs at him and he runs off.

ELLIOTT: *Oh, God!*

GRETA *is left standing alone, with a pile of presents in her arms. She's stunned and shell-shocked, breathing heavily.*

GRETA: So … many … people …

GENEVIEVE *rushes through.*

GENEVIEVE: What are you doing in here?

GRETA: I'm coming … I'll be down there in a sec.

GENEVIEVE *looks at* GRETA.

GENEVIEVE: Are you okay? You're looking a little peaky.

GRETA: No … I'm fine.

GENEVIEVE: Are you sure?

GRETA: Of course not. I'll just … I'll just take these to my room first.

GENEVIEVE: Alright. But if you're not downstairs in two minutes time I'm going to hunt you down and drag you down there myself, idiot.

JANET *calls out from the other room.*

JANET: [*off*] *Who wants baby quiches?!*

GENEVIEVE: God help us! Those baby quiches!

GENEVIEVE *runs back into the fray of the party.*

GRETA *picks up all the presents and, balancing them in her arms, goes back to her room.*

She throws the presents onto her bed.

She jumps in fright as she discovers UMBER *standing in her room.*

GRETA: I didn't hear you come in. You gave me a fright.

They have a very weird and extended face-off. Eventually GRETA *crumbles.*

Can I get you a punch or something?

UMBER *moves further into the room and* JADE *saunters in behind her, casting her eyes around the bedroom, taking it all in.*

Jade! Hi. You're here too!

JADE: To be completely honest, we were a bit surprised when we received our invitation. Weren't we, Umber?

> JADE *looks at* UMBER, *but* UMBER *doesn't respond at all. She just stares at* GRETA.

See, we were under the impression that you had no interest in us. You know, as friends.

GRETA: What? Why would you think that?

JADE: We offered you an olive branch of friendship, and when you didn't snap it up straight away we were a little ... how would you put it, Umber?

> *She says nothing.*

You just totally read my mind. Miffed. We were a little miffed.

GRETA: ... Miffed?

JADE: Miffed. Dismayed. Perturbed. The last one's an adjective.

GRETA: Really?

JADE: You've been totally avoiding us. It's abnormal, you know, that's how we noticed. It upset us. Didn't it, Umber?

> UMBER *doesn't respond.*

GRETA: I'm so sorry. I had no idea that was how you guys felt. If I'd known I would have just ... I dunno. Invited you over to hang out ... more often ... or something.

JADE: What? Like in your room?

> JADE *casts her eyes over the room.*

GRETA: Yeah. For sure.

JADE: Really? You're not just saying it.

GRETA: No way! Why wouldn't I? You guys are so nice, you've only ever said nice things to me.

JADE: Well, yeah. That is true. We have only said nice things. Umber?

> UMBER *holds out the present for* GRETA *to take.* GRETA *has to come and take it out of her hand.*

This is for you?

GRETA: A birthday present?

JADE: Well, it is your birthday, isn't it?

GRETA: Yeah, true. Thanks.

JADE: Don't open it now. Save it for later. When you're ... alone.

GRETA: Sure. Okay.

JADE: You're so welcome.

> GRETA *puts the present aside.*
>
> *They fall into a silence.*
>
> *The twins look at the room.*

GRETA: It's really nice of you guys to come over. And thank you so so so much for the present. Seriously. I mean it.

> *The twins look to each other.*
>
> *They both attempt to stifle a laugh.*
>
> UMBER *shakes her head as if to say, 'Don't say it'.*

… What?

> *They pull themselves together, both trying to hide their smirks.*

What's so funny?

JADE: Nothing.

> *Pause.*

… Nice room.

> *They both stare at* GRETA, *trying to hold in their laughs.*
>
> *Blackout.*

♦ ♦ ♦ ♦ ♦ ♦ ♦ ♦ ♦ ♦

In the darkness we hear a tape recording. It's something that was home-made on a cassette deck.

We hear JADE*'s voice.*

JADE: Is it recording? Okay. Right. Are you ready? Okay. So. Greta. This is Jade and Umber, which as if you couldn't already tell. It's your birthday, which also as if you couldn't already tell.

> *Giggles are heard in the background, but not from one voice. From quite a few.* JADE *shushes them, and more shushes can be heard.*
>
> *The lights slowly start to come up to reveal* GRETA *sitting in front of her stereo, the tape playing in the cassette deck. The wrapping from Jade and Umber's present is in her hands.*

We know you're kind of new around here, but we also know you like to keep to yourself. You're a private kind of person, and that's cool, you know. To each their own. So Umber said, 'What could we give Greta for her fifteenth birthday that no-one else will ever give her?' And I said, 'I know. A song. Let's give her a song.' So here's a song. We wrote this one ourself. Ready, Umber? Okay.

The following song is terrible and juvenile and doesn't rhyme, like it's done by someone with no musicality whatsoever. It's horrible and wrong and awkward.

JADE & UMBER: [*together, singing*]
    You've got no tits.
    You've got no tits.
    No-one will touch your bits.
    You think you're so good,
    You're a frigid bitch, and your friend is a homo.
    Your face looks like a pig,
    And you wear clothes that make you look like a twelve-year-old boy.
    You've got no tits.
    You've got no tits.
    No-one will touch your bits.

Throughout, lots of people can be heard laughing in the background.

The song ends.

People cheer in the background.

That's for ignoring me and my sister. We could have been your friends. Happy birthday. Hope you have a swell time. Bitch.

GUEST 1: [*laughing*] She's got no tits! Seriously! She doesn't!

GUEST 2: She sounds like a guy when she talks! Have you heard? No wonder she doesn't say much.

GUEST 3: [*laughing*] That is so harsh!

The tape ends.

GRETA *is silent. Tears running down her face. She sits in silence for a while, then reaches out and calmly presses the eject button, and takes the cassette out. She sits with it in her hand for a while, just staring at it in disbelief.*

Suddenly there's a knock on the door.

GRETA: [*calling out*] Just a second!

She wipes her eyes and straightens herself up.

She sits back on the bed, gathering herself. Taking a deep breath.

[*Calling out*] Come in!

The door opens and ELLIOTT *comes in. We hear the sound of the party momentarily as he steps into the room, closing the door behind him.*

ELLIOTT: What are you doing in here? Everyone's been looking for you. It's your party, you know.

GRETA: Yeah, I know. I just needed a breather. Thought I'd put my presents up here …

ELLIOTT: Man, you so scored tonight! Look at this haul. You got a mixed tape! That's an awesome present! What's on it?

She looks at the cassette in her hands.

GRETA: Oh … you know. Just the usual stuff.

Awkward pause.

ELLIOTT: … Greta. You know before how I said I wanted to talk to you about something?

She looks up at him.

I don't know if this is the right time to bring it up but … Well, you know you're my best friend. You are totally my best friend.

GRETA: Yeah?

ELLIOTT: Well, do you … I'm your best friend too, aren't I?

GRETA: You're my only friend, Elliott.

ELLIOTT: That's not true. You're actually popular. Even the twins are here. Go downstairs and see for yourself.

GRETA *looks at him suspiciously.*

Well … it doesn't matter … God, what am I trying to say? You're my best friend, and I'd never want to risk our friendship.

GRETA: Yeah …?

ELLIOTT: … I'd never want to risk our friendship … But some things, they're worth risking.

Beat.

GRETA: What are you saying?

ELLIOTT: … I want you to be more than just a friend …

> *Pause.*

You look amazing tonight.

> GRETA *recoils.*

GRETA: … What are you doing …?

ELLIOTT: I've been feeling this way for a while, but when I saw you tonight in that dress …

GRETA: Elliott …? What are you doing? What the fuck are you doing?

ELLIOTT: … I'm just telling you how I feel.

> GRETA *is dumbstruck.*

Say something, will you?

GRETA: What? What do you want me to say?

ELLIOTT: Umm … that you want to be more than friends too.

GRETA: Why? Why would I do that?

ELLIOTT: I dunno … I just thought, 'cause we'd been hanging out so much lately.

GRETA: Oh, you 'thought', did you? You 'thought' you'd just come in here and I'd throw myself at your feet. Is that it?

ELLIOTT: Jesus, Greta. That's a bit harsh. I'm just saying.

GRETA: Go on. Tell me I'm being a frigid bitch. That's what you really want to say, isn't it?

ELLIOTT: Greta …?

GRETA: Everyone says you're a homo anyway, why would I even be interested in someone like you?

> ELLIOTT *looks at her, completely stunned.*

Go on. Tell me I'm a bitch! I know you're thinking it!

> *He turns and runs from the room.*

> GRETA *can't believe what just came out of her mouth.*

Greta? What are you doing?

> *She buries her head in her hands.*

> *The music from downstairs starts to get louder, and she covers her ears. It's all becoming too much.*

Make it stop … please, make it all just stop! *Now!*

Suddenly her music box pops open and starts to play, and the curtain blows into the room. GRETA *is a little freaked by it. She gets up and shuts the music box and the wind dies down instantly. She looks to the window.*

What the hell?

She pulls out her key and locks the music box.

As she turns to leave the room ...

[*Calling*] Elliott!

She is stopped dead in her tracks once more.

An old CRONE *is standing in her doorway. She is completely hidden under layers of clothing and long hair.*

She just stares silently at GRETA. *It's creepy.*

Hello ...

The CRONE *says nothing.*

... Tonight wasn't supposed to be fancy dress ...

She still doesn't answer.

Everyone's downstairs in the rumpus room if you wanna go down there ...

The CRONE *shakes her head from side to side.*

... Umm you know what, I have to find my friend. I'm just going to head down ...

As GRETA *takes a step to head out of the room, everything snaps into slow motion. The* CRONE's *arms extend until they are unnaturally long, reaching across the room to grab* GRETA's *music box. They retract and she now has it firmly in her grasp.*

As she takes the box GRETA *retracts her hand in pain. A large splinter from the music box lodged firmly in her hand.*

The CRONE *turns and escapes.*

Everything really starts to warp and bend. The sound of the party starts to sound like it's underwater.

GRETA *starts to stagger, like she is drugged.*

Slowly her eyes begin to close.

She is starting to fall asleep.

She sinks slowly down onto her bed.

We can hear the sound of her falling gathering speed like a meteor as it enters the atmosphere. It builds in intensity until we hear the sound of GRETA *hitting the ground with an almighty impact.*

◆ ◆ ◆ ◆ ◆ ◆ ◆ ◆ ◆ ◆

The lights come up again to reveal GRETA *laying on the ground. Her room no longer there.*

The place is cold and mysterious now. She's in another world.

A piece of origami flicks and flitters into the space. A crane.

It flicks around, eventually landing on her face. It tickles her nose.

GRETA, *still seemingly asleep, tries to brush it away with her hand. It keeps persisting. She brushes it away a second time.*

She opens her eyes, still kind of asleep.

Suddenly she sits bolt upright, like she's just had a bucket of water thrown on her face. Figuratively speaking.

She looks around at her surroundings. She has no idea where she is.

GRETA: Where am I? … *Elliott?!*

> *She goes to get up, but winces suddenly at a pain in her hand.*
>
> *The origami, which is now on the ground alongside her, tries to get her attention. It either makes a little rustling sound, or a little whistle.*
>
> GRETA *hears this but has no idea where it's coming from. She looks around, but sees nothing. It rustles again. This time she sees it. It moves and she gets a huge fright.*

Oh, my God …

> *It moves again and she squeals.*

Eeeekkk!

> *It rustles once more and she finally recognises it.*

… Paper crane …?

> *It rustles again.*

Greta …? Is that you …?

It rustles a yes.

GRETA *picks it up and starts to unfold the paper, being incredibly gentle with it.*

Once the paper opens out, FINNISH GRETA *appears. Breathing heavily like she's just been released from a car after an accident. She is a giant piece of paper, or a national costume.*

FINN GRETA: Oh, my word, Greta, I can't tell you how horribly terrifying that was. One minute I was in your room, with all our other correspondences, the party was in full swing downstairs, when suddenly we were falling and I could feel my stomach in my mouth and I knew that when we hit the ground it was going to be so terribly horrifically terrifying that I saw my life in Helsinki flash before my eyes /

GRETA: Greta, oh, my dearest Greta. Just slow down. Take a deep breath and calm down. Just calm down.

FINN GRETA *takes a deep breath and tries to calm, which she eventually does.*

Better?

FINN GRETA: Yes, thanking you, Greta. Much better.

GRETA: Now. First things first, Greta. We're not in my room anymore. Do you know where we are?

FINN GRETA: Do I know where we are? In a word, Greta? No. I have no idea. You?

GRETA: I have no idea either.

FINN GRETA: Oh, great! That's just fantastic. We could be anywhere! This is so much worse than that time when I ended up in the dead letter office because of a stupid spelling mistake that left me somewhere on the outskirts of Vienna. Australia! Australia! Not Austria-la.

GRETA: Don't get upset. I'm sure … there must be some kind of logical explanation to all this.

FINN GRETA: Logic! This is the thinking we need, dearest Greta. One step in the backwards time.

GRETA: My music box … I think …

A tiny whinny can be heard in the distance.

FINN GRETA: What was that? Greta, what was that sound?

GRETA: It sounded like a … like a …

We hear the sound again.

Like a whinny …

FINN GRETA: Look! Over there!

A tiny plastic horse appears. It gallops into the space and stops.

GRETA: Plastic horses? One of my plastic horses?

It neighs.

FINN GRETA: I think he's trying to tell us something.

The horse neighs and whinnies again.

GRETA: I'm sorry, plastic horse. I can't understand you. I don't know what you're trying to say.

It neighs.

FINN GRETA: What? Really?

It whinnies.

I can only just … what? Speak up please!

Neighing continues intermittently through FINN GRETA *'s dialogue.*

Yes … Yes … Okay … Yes … No … You don't say … Apparently we are in the trouble. There are hunters here. And they are hunting you!

GRETA: Hunting me? Are you serious?

FINN GRETA: Horses never joke. You know that's not possible, Greta.

GRETA: So what am I supposed to do?

FINN GRETA: You need to find the maiden with the tiny hands. She is the only one who can release you from this realm.

GRETA: The maiden with tiny hands?

A shadow passes over the back of the space and a horrible shrieking can be heard in the distance. And the sound of metal blades spinning.

FINN GRETA: Oh, my … What is that …?

The horse neighs again and starts to move away.

He's telling us we need to move. The hunters are approaching. And they will take no prisoners.

GRETA: What should we do?

FINN GRETA: Jump on his back?

> *There's a flash of light, and then we're plunged into darkness for a moment.*

Jump on *his* back.

> *When the lights come back up, the horse is no longer tiny. It is full-sized.*

> GRETA *climbs onto its back.*

Lead us to safety, majestic creature.

> *They start to gallop. They gallop for what seems an eternity.*

Follow the river.

GRETA: He's taking us towards the forest.

FINN GRETA: Oh, my word. How exhilarating.

> *They keep riding.*

GRETA: He's leading us deeper into the forest.

FINN GRETA: Ride, stallion. Ride.

GRETA: Up ahead! There's a bridge!

FINN GRETA: Yes. I see it.

GRETA: We should cross.

> *They cross.*

FINN GRETA: We should cross further.

> *The sound of the terrors starts to emerge again.*

Quick. The hunters must be near. I will look from above.

> *They gallop further. Then suddenly* FINN GRETA *calls out.*

Greta! The bridge! It's a trap! I can see the hunters. You must stop the horse. Tell him to stop!

GRETA: Stop! Please stop, horse! Greta … he doesn't understand me!

FINN GRETA: I don't want to die, Greta! I don't want to die!

GRETA: This can't be it. It can't end like this …

> GRETA *looks up to the sky. The sound of wings is approaching.*

What's that? In the sky? *Watch out!*

> *The horse whinnies furiously as they collide with the bridge, and are met with an enormous explosion.*

> *Blackout.*

♦ ♦ ♦ ♦ ♦ ♦ ♦ ♦ ♦ ♦

GRETA *comes to.*

GRETA: Where am I?

For the first time GRETA *sees who saved her.*

She can't take her eyes off her. It's GENEVIEVE *as a giant* FIREBIRD.

FIREBIRD: Somewhere safe, dick brains. If you think being with me is safe.

A cold wind passes through and she yells out to it. She grabs GRETA.

Are you happy now?! She can't even fend for herself because of you!

The wind subsides. And the FIREBIRD *lets go of* GRETA, *who scurries away. She throws her a piece of food.*

Eat this. You're gonna need your strength.

The sound can be heard in the distance again, travelling on the wind. The FIREBIRD *yells out to it angrily again.*

Get off my mountain, bitch lips!

It sounds faintly like someone crying, and the tinkling of ice crystals. GRETA *starts to shake, like the air has suddenly chilled around them. The* FIREBIRD *hardens in her resolve.*

GRETA: Who are you talking to?
FIREBIRD: The queen, shit pants. Who do you think?

Pause.

GRETA: Someone stole something from me.
FIREBIRD: I know.
GRETA: I need to get it back.
FIREBIRD: And you expect me to help?

Beat.

You have no idea what you're asking, do you? You're not ready to go back out there. You're not ready to face those hunters. You're still just a little girl.
GRETA: I am not.
FIREBIRD: A helpless little baby.

GRETA: Don't call me that!

FIREBIRD: What a dumb little bubba wubba.

GRETA: Shut up.

FIREBIRD: Make me, crap smear.

The sound of the hunters starts to be heard in the distance.

GRETA: Please. I'm begging you. I can't leave without it. I need you to help me.

ELLIOTT *appears for a moment. The sound of the party drifts in. He bangs on an approximation of where her door would be, and calls out.*

ELLIOTT: Greta … Greta! Are you still in there?! What are you doing?! You can't stay in your room all night. I heard about what the twins did … Greta?!

GRETA: … Elliott … ?!

As ELLIOTT *fades away again the* FIREBIRD *snaps at* GRETA.

FIREBIRD: Call her name. Only the queen can help you now. But you have been warned.

The FIREBIRD *whispers something in her ear.*

GRETA: What?

FIREBIRD: Invoke her one true name. But do it backwards! Do it. Now!

GRETA *strikes the ground with her foot three times.*

GRETA: *Tenaj! Tenaj! Tenaj!*

The ground opens up, and the trumpets of hell sound. A rumbling sound emerges from within like the groan of a stone giant waking from a thousand-year slumber.

The FIREBIRD *plucks a feather from his body and hands it to* GRETA.

FIREBIRD: Take this. Her cave is without warmth or light. Breathe on it and you'll soon find your way. You're an idiot. I don't envy the pain you'll soon feel. Suck my balls.

GRETA *goes to step into the hole, and the* FIREBIRD *prepares to take off as the sound of the terrors sweeps through.*

Blackout.

In the darkness we are suddenly inside a vast chamber. A cold wind blows through it. Ice crystals can be heard tinkling in the cold emptiness.

A moan can be heard in the darkness. It sounds like someone who has cried and cried and cried, but can cry no more.

A gentle blowing can be heard in the darkness. After a few breaths, we can make out the figure of GRETA. *She is breathing on the feather, which gently illuminates the room, ebbing and flowing with each breath.*

She gives it one last blow, and seeing a jar on the ground, places the feather inside. The room, even though it is cast in shadows, starts to become brighter.

A large figure begins to stir in the shadows, like a small hill that is coming to life. A dark brooding creature who would terrify even the bravest of souls.

QUEEN: Who dares disturb my sorrow?

GRETA: So ... cold ...

QUEEN: Do you have any idea what I could do to you?

> *Beat.*

> *The* QUEEN *looks down to her hands. A smashed music box in her grasp.* GRETA *reaches for it.*

Looking for this?

> GRETA *reaches out and grabs the broken music box.*

GRETA: It's not mine. Why did you break it?

QUEEN: Because it was not the right one, was it?

> *A sad glint appears in her eyes.*

It was not the beautiful song. The one I remember from my youth. Full of promise and grace ... and love.

> *The* QUEEN *gets lost in this thought for a moment, then turns her focus back on* GRETA.

Us.

> *She reaches out towards* GRETA *who suddenly starts to freeze.*

GRETA: What are you doing to me?

QUEEN: You're just like me now. Just like me.

> *A cold wind starts to rush towards* GRETA, *growing louder and louder.*

GRETA: Oh God … please … please … don't hurt me …!

QUEEN: Prepare to feel my arctic chill …

The QUEEN *starts to breath in. It is like she is sucking a tonne of air into her lungs.*

As she is about to exhale, GRETA *starts to sing the tune of her song and the* QUEEN *stops dead in her tracks.*

She starts to cry joyous tears, and begins to melt. Warmth creeps back into her hardened heart.

She hears the song out, dropping back down onto her throne.

The QUEEN *can hardly even speak.*

My song …? That's my song!

GRETA: Yeah. It's my song too.

The QUEEN *can hardly speak.*

QUEEN: You will bring it to me!

GRETA: But I can't. It was stolen by a horrible witch.

The QUEEN *looks at her.*

You know her. Don't you?

She nods.

How do I find her?

QUEEN: She lives in a tiny house, at the centre of a maze.

The sound of the terrors is heard in the distance again.

Guarding the entrance is the foulest of creatures. A pitiful slag of a worm. A vile, despicable goblin. But he'll never let you pass beyond into the labyrinth to his beloved.

GRETA: He'll have to, 'cause if that witch ever wants to listen to my music box, she can't do it without this.

She takes the key from around her neck.

The QUEEN*'s eyes light up.*

I'll make you a deal. If you show me where this maze is …

QUEEN: Then I will let you live.

GRETA *thinks about this for a moment as the terrors outside grow more intense.*

GRETA: But how will I make it past those hunters?

QUEEN: Past them is not the way you must go. There is only one way to find the entrance to the great maze. That is … through my mouth.

GRETA: Through your mouth.

QUEEN: Yes. Through my mouth. You will travel through my spit. Because the only way to find the hideous goblin is through my phlegm and bile.

> GRETA *is horrified at the prospect. She hears the terrors approaching closer.*

GRETA: Oh God … Seriously?

> *The* QUEEN *starts to hack up a goober.* GRETA *winces with each protracted hack.*

Oh God.

QUEEN: Just … [*hack*] … give me a … [*hack*] … second … [*hack*] … I'm a bit dry today … [*hack, hack, hack*] … that's getting there … [*hack*] … I just need … [hack] … a full … [*hack*] … like a decent … [*hack*] … mouthful … [*hack*] … of phlegm … oh, yeah … [*hack*] … that's the ticket … [*hack*] … like a fat oyster … [*hack*]

> GRETA *is totally repulsed.*

What …? You never seen … a grown woman's bodily … fluids before?

> GRETA *flinches as the* QUEEN *attempts to speak through a mouthful of spit.*

Alright. Ready. Get in. C'mon. Mumma's got you!

> *She opens her mouth wide.*

GRETA: … I can't believe I'm doing this …

> *The* QUEEN *grunts at her impatiently with her mouth wide open.*

> GRETA *cautiously walks towards her and starts to put her hand inside her mouth. She squeals with utter repulsion and disgust.*

> *Blackout.*

◆ ◆ ◆ ◆ ◆ ◆ ◆ ◆ ◆

The lights come up again.
The QUEEN *and her throne room have disappeared.*
The sound of a missile/projectile flying through the air.

GRETA *lands with a loud sloppy splat. Her head covered in phlegmy slime. A gate/doorway is in front of her.*

GRETA *tries to open it but can't.*

The GOBLIN *appears from nowhere and* GRETA *jumps back in fear.*

He steps towards the gate, and takes up his position as sentry.

GRETA: Open this gate. I need to pass.

> *The* GOBLIN *ignores her.*

I said open this gate immediately.

> *She stomps her foot.*

GOBLIN: Ask nice.

GRETA: Will you please open the gate?

> *The* GOBLIN *thinks about this for a moment.*

GOBLIN: Mmmm. No.

> GRETA *lunges at the gate. But it's locked tight.*

You think gate open so easy? You dumb.

GRETA: Well, you're mean.

GOBLIN: But me pretty though, don't you think? Don't you think I look like handsome pretty man?

GRETA: Oh my God, I'm gonna be sick.

GOBLIN: See my body? Made of spit. Made of slobber and drool. Meanie queenie been gobbing on me for years.

GRETA: She spits on you! Why?

GOBLIN: Listen to this … have you heard the one about the police who were called to a day care centre?

GRETA: Ummm … no.

GOBLIN: The three-year-old was resisting a rest.

> GRETA *smirks.*

You think me is funny, yes?

GRETA: Maybe.

GOBLIN: She not find funny. She did once, but no more. I tell you a secret, though. Come closer. I whisper …

> GRETA *edges in cautiously, but she's growing fond of this idiot.*

Secret is … I don't mind. I actually like the gobble juice.

GRETA *recoils at this.*

GRETA: That's disgusting!

The GOBLIN *hacks up a goober and spits on himself as well.*

GOBLIN: Queenie think she did first spit on goblin, but she wrong. Goblin been spitting on himself forever. Since beginning of everything.

GRETA *looks at the* GOBLIN *for a moment.*

GRETA: Goblin. Let me through that gate?

GOBLIN: You no go there. Lovely young girlies go into this gate and never come out the same again. They come out changed. They come out broken.

GRETA: But I have no choice. My music box is in there.

The sound of the terrors starts to approach again. The GOBLIN *looks around in fear.*

That sound. You know what that sound is, don't you?

GOBLIN: That the hunters. They almost here.

GRETA: Open this gate then. Please!

GOBLIN: What did the rude prism say to the beam that bumped into him?

GRETA: Now is not the time for jokes! Open the gate!

GOBLIN: Get bent.

GRETA: Stop it! You have to stop it now!

GOBLIN: … What about this one? Have you seen that new movie? What's it called again? What's it called?

GRETA: I'll be careful, Dad. You have to trust me.

The door opens and GRETA *goes through it.*

GOBLIN: *You be broken now, Greta Driscoll! You be broken forever! Princess Greta not change yet! Not break yet! Please!*

Suddenly the GOBLIN *hears the sound of invisible creatures darting around him. They are everywhere. He starts to panic.*

No … No …

The sound of the terrors wheels towards him with ferocious speed, as he shields his face from the attack.

No!

Blackout.

♦ ♦ ♦ ♦ ♦ ♦ ♦ ♦ ♦ ♦

GRETA *is all alone.*

She is standing in the middle of a misty moor. It is cold and strange.

The sound of the birthday party starts to emerge. She can hear teenagers yelling out and music playing, but it's like it's distant. Like it's under water.

DENISE MACKELL *runs through. Calling out for* ELLIOTT.

Another teenager runs to the corner and vomits.

Another dances through. It's slow and sexy and weird.

GRETA *watches all this like she's in a dream.*

She starts to hear the scratching of a record in the distance that has reached the end of the side.

A record player and some stacks of records appear. It's playing but it is at the end of its side. There's a sign stuck to the lid of the turntable, which GRETA *reads.*

GRETA: 'Turn me on'?

> *She turns over the vinyl, putting down the needle.*

> *A seventies style soundtrack comes on again,* à la *Serge Gainsbourg.*

> SERGE *appears from behind the record player.*

SERGE: *Bonjour*, Greta.

GRETA: Serge Gainsbourg …?

SERGE: *Oui. C'est moi.*

GRETA: I'm sorry … I don't understand French.

SERGE: And I don't understand English.

GRETA: What …? But you just said—

SERGE: Sorry, Greta, but this is my humour.

GRETA: Oh … Okay.

SERGE: Crazy party, huh. Lucky you fell asleep.

GRETA: Me?

SERGE: Yes, you! You are in the snooze mode. I don't blame you. Birthdays can be hell. *Merde! Encules!*

GRETA: Really? … I'm asleep?

SERGE: *Oui. Vous dormez comme un bébé.* Like a baby.

GRETA: But I have to find the witch. I have to get my music box back.

SERGE: Greta, don't be ridiculous … nothing is happening. You have not lost a thing.

GRETA *looks around.*

GRETA: Where are we then?

SERGE: We're in your bedroom! Just you and me …

He starts to dance a little.

GRETA: But I don't understand. I can't be asleep. I need to find my song.

SERGE: Oh, *ma petite.* Don't worry your head about it. That song is no good to you anymore. Listen to me. This song, my song can be yours now. All yours, *mon amour.*

It's like he's casting a spell on GRETA. *The space starts to fill with smoke, it shoots from his finger, like he's drugging her.*

GRETA: Your song …? But I don't want your song. I want my own.

SERGE: You look so beautiful in that dress.

The song changes and something even sexier/sleazier kicks in.

Ooooo. Track two. Now we are talking! Such an incredible beauty. I can hardly contain my desires when I see such a beautiful woman.

GRETA: This is making me feel uncomfortable.

SERGE: Greta … do you feel it too? I know you do. You feel it, just like I feel it.

She looks at him … she's had this conversation before.

You're my best friend, and I'd never want to risk our friendship …

GRETA: Whoa … what the hell is happening here?

SERGE*'s accent starts to slip and he starts to sound more and more like* ELLIOTT.

SERGE: I want you to be more than just a friend. You look amazing tonight, Greta.

He starts to advance on her and she backs away.

I want to touch you. I want to touch you all over. I want to be your first.

GRETA: This isn't happening.

SERGE: I want to kiss you and touch you and make sweet, sweet love.

The music kicks in louder. He dances towards her. She finds herself in a creepy slow dance with him.

GRETA: This is not happening! You're not Elliott! He wouldn't do this. Not to me.

SERGE: Shhh. Listen to your new song, Greta. Feel it in your heart, feel it in your body …

She tears herself from him and rips the needle from the record player.

GRETA: No … no … I don't want this …

SERGE *puts the needle back on the player and is again all over her in an instant.*

SERGE: You came through the gate, Greta. You wanted to be here.

GRETA: Fuck you.

SERGE: Only if you ask nice.

He advances on her.

Now I'm going to make you a woman.

She gets to the record player and pulls it off again.

SERGE *waves his finger at her.*

He puts the needle down on the same record again, but this time a different track starts up. It's the song that JADE *and* UMBER *made* GRETA.

You have made them angry, Greta. You should not have done that that that that …

SERGE *disappears into the mist.*

The music starts to bend and twist as it changes into a strange foreboding sound. The sound of the terrors.

They enter the space finally. They are the horror versions of JADE *and* UMBER. *Fierce and terrifying. The sound of the terrors twists and changes until we start to hear the tape once more. The song they made for her.*

GRETA: You? You're the hunters?

UMBER *opens her mouth and a howl emerges.*

I don't care what you do to me. Bring it on, bitches.

The twins and GRETA *face off from across the room. They suddenly charge at one another. As they are about to collide there's a shattering explosion.*

Blackout.

♦ ♦ ♦ ♦ ♦ ♦ ♦ ♦ ♦ ♦

The lights come back up to reveal GRETA *standing over the bodies of the twins.*

A small doorway to a small house has appeared. The light turns on inside.

GRETA *looks at the house. She looks at the bodies of the twins. She turns back to the house and crawls through the door.*

The house turns around to reveal what looks like her bedroom. But standing in the middle of it is the CRONE.

She is holding GRETA'*s music box in her hands.*

They look at each other for a moment.

GRETA: Did I do something to you? Did I do something that made you hate me?

The CRONE *slowly shakes her head 'No'.*

Why did you do it then? Why did you send me to sleep? Why did you steal the only thing I love?

The CRONE *points to the key around* GRETA'*s neck.*

GRETA *looks down at it.*

This? You want this?

The CRONE *nods slowly.*

Well, guess what? You can't have it. Do you wanna know why? 'Cause it's mine. That music box belongs to me. Not you. Do you hear me? It's mine.

The CRONE *looks down towards the ground, like she's saddened.*

So give it back to me. Now. Give it back! *Give it back! Now!*

GRETA *lunges at the box and grabs it from her hands ... but the* CRONE'*s hands come with it.* GRETA *looks at the hands in shock. She can't believe what just happened.*

The CRONE *looks at* GRETA *for a moment, then slowly starts to take off her cloak, and then her large head.*

The CRONE *is a child. The eight-year-old version of* GRETA *from the picture on her wall. She quietly looks to* GRETA.

Me? You're me?

LITTLE GRETA *nods.*

This … all this … it was you?

LITTLE GRETA: No, silly. It was you.

She points to the music box.

If you let me have it, I'll help you wake up. Promise.

GRETA *thinks about this for a moment.*

She hands the key over to her.

LITTLE GRETA *grabs the key, opens the box, and plays the music for a moment.*

She smiles, getting lost for a moment in the song.

Give me your hand.

GRETA *gives her her hand.*

You've got a splinter.

GRETA: The maiden with the tiny hands …

LITTLE GRETA: Got it.

GRETA *starts to hear a whistling sound as the lights fade.*

◆ ◆ ◆ ◆ ◆ ◆ ◆ ◆ ◆

Greta's bedroom is back to normal again. GRETA *is laying on the bed, still asleep.*

GENEVIEVE *sits over her. The party can be still heard downstairs.*

GENEVIEVE: [*softly*] Hey. Greta?

She gently closes the door behind her and steps over to the bed quietly, sitting alongside her.

Greta. Wake up.

After a few moments, GRETA *begins to stir.*

Slowly she sits up.

She looks around the room, bleary eyed.

She looks at the presents on the floor.

Then she looks to her sister.

GRETA *doesn't know what to say.*

Are you okay?

Pause.

Elliott told me about the cassette.

GRETA *gives her a look.*

GRETA: They called me a frigid bitch. They've turned everyone against me.

GENEVIEVE: If you believe it, then yeah, they have.

GRETA: But I did nothing to them.

GENEVIEVE: I know. But they're nasty, and they're scared. They're scared of not being beautiful. They're scared of not being popular. They're scared of what will happen when someone who they fear becomes an incredible woman and just totally overtakes them.

GRETA: … That's not going to happen.

GENEVIEVE: Greta. It already has.

She takes a deep breath.

You remember a few years ago, around when I was turning fifteen?

GRETA: Yeah.

GENEVIEVE: And I stopped talking to you.

GRETA *laughs.*

GRETA: Yes. Vividly.

GENEVIEVE: And I cut my hair off. And Mum didn't know what to do. She used to freak constantly, she used to say to Dad that she was at her wit's end and that she didn't know where her little girl had disappeared to. You remember?

GRETA *doesn't say anything.*

You know, nothing ever actually happened to me. Nothing bad … I just woke up one morning and I knew I was different. I realised that the world was bigger than me and us … and it took me a while. It was like a new person had turned up inside my body and just kicked the old one out. And it wasn't easy. I was angry. I still am sometimes.

GRETA: Yeah, no shit, Sherlock.

GENEVIEVE gives her a look.

GENEVIEVE: Look, all this … it's just my way of saying that what you're going through now … I know it's shit, and I know it's confusing and you're pretty much hating it, but you're not alone. And as long as I'm around, you never will be. Alright?

GRETA: … Alright.

GENEVIEVE: Just don't get used to me being nice to you in public though. I've got a reputation to uphold.

GRETA: Alright. Deal.

A cheer can be heard from downstairs.

GENEVIEVE: Right. We better get downstairs. But first …

She picks up the cassette and the wrapping paper, wrapping it back up and holding it out to GRETA.

This. This never existed!

She puts it in her pocket.

GRETA: But what about Jade and Umber?

GENEVIEVE: The Hunter twins? They're about to get busted by their parents for bringing booze tonight in three, two, one.

The two girls' pleading cries can be heard in the distance, along with an adult yelling angrily.

GRETA: Thank you, Gen. Seriously.

A knock can be heard on the door. ELLIOTT *pokes his head in.*

GENEVIEVE *puts on a mock angry big sister voice.*

GENEVIEVE: Then you can't stay in your room all night for all I care, you little turd muncher.

ELLIOTT *isn't sure what's going on. He's about to leave when* GENEVIEVE *suddenly picks up something from the floor and throws it half-heartedly at* GRETA*'s head.*

ELLIOTT: Jesus! Big sister, take it easy, alright! She's had a hard enough night as it is.

GENEVIEVE *leaves and* GRETA *calls out to her, trying to be tough too, but is very bad at it.*

GRETA: Yeah! Get out, you slapper, before I … slap your arse … face …

ELLIOTT *is a bit shocked.*

ELLIOTT: You guys are so emotive.
GRETA: Yeah. It's genetic.
ELLIOTT: Generic?
GRETA: No. Genetic.
ELLIOTT: Oh. That makes more sense.

Awkward pause.

They both go to speak at the same time.

GRETA: Look, about before /
ELLIOTT: That was pretty /
GRETA: Sorry … you go first.

ELLIOTT *gathers himself for a moment.*

ELLIOTT: Okay! You had no right to call me a homo before.

GRETA *doesn't say anything.*

I mean, there's absolutely nothing wrong with being gay, I'd be totally fine if I was, but the point is: A) I don't you think you meant it as a compliment, and B) I actually do like girls. I dream about them all the time. I think about them way too much. I look at chicks like there's no tomorrow. At least six or seven times a day I think about them and I have a / …
GRETA: Alright. I think I got that point already.
ELLIOTT: Right. Good … Which brings me to my next point, which was that I declared my … interest for you.
GRETA: And I'm sorry for what I said. It was cruel.
ELLIOTT: Right … well … I was going to … make that point too … which I'm glad … that you've also made, already, I wasn't expecting that …
GRETA: Elliott …?
ELLIOTT: Yes, well … I had no right to spring that on you. It's your birthday. You don't need nasty surprises like that on your birthday. No-one does.
GRETA: Whoa. Hold on a sec.
ELLIOTT: Hold on a sec what?

GRETA: You had every right.

ELLIOTT: … I did?

GRETA: Why wouldn't you? You were just telling me how you feel, yeah?

ELLIOTT: … Yeah.

GRETA: You're my best friend.

ELLIOTT: That's what I thought.

GRETA: But I need you to understand, though, that … right now … you being my best friend is the best thing in the world to me. You are so so so close to my heart.

> ELLIOTT *thinks about this for a moment.*

ELLIOTT: But what I said … that kinda changes things now though, doesn't it? Between us.

GRETA: Yeah. But that's okay, isn't it?

> ELLIOTT *thinks about it a bit more.*

If you find it too hard to be my friend now I will respect your decision five hundred per cent.

> ELLIOTT *thinks about this for a moment.*

ELLIOTT: That dress is so nice.

GRETA: Elliott … please, don't …

ELLIOTT: No, let me speak. I think that dress is so nice that I'd like to wear it. Downstairs. And you know how you said before … about how much you would have rather worn my suit …? So how about it? A breeze down below will be quite refreshing for me.

> GRETA *looks at him for a moment, not sure if he's being serious …*

GRETA: Everyone's going to laugh at us.

ELLIOTT: I know. It's going to be awesome.

> *A huge smile breaks across* GRETA*'s face and the two of them swap outfits.*
>
> *They both look hilarious.*
>
> *A breezy, romantic seventies pop song starts up downstairs.*
>
> GRETA *reaches up and kisses him.*

What was that for?

GRETA: I'm glad you're my friend.

> *Pause.*

ELLIOTT: Me too. Good friends.
GRETA: Great friends.

> *A smile breaks across both their faces.*

> JANET *pokes her head in. She's carrying a cupcake with an unlit candle.*

JANET: There you are, you little carrot! What in God's name …?
GRETA: … We were just /
ELLIOTT: We've been all over the place. She's been the most incredible social butterfly tonight, Janet. You would've hardly recognised her.
JANET: Yes, well, I can see that, Elliott … and I'm Mrs Driscoll to you, thank you very much …
ELLIOTT: No worries, Janet.

> JANET *tuts at him.*

> CONRAD *bursts in.*

CONRAD: Did you find— He's wearing a dress!
ELLIOTT: Hey, Conrad. Fabulous party. You're an awesome host.
CONRAD: He's wearing a dress!
JANET: Did you find the matches?
ELLIOTT: I'll take care of it, Janet. They're in the pantry under the sparklers and the Soda Stream refills, you silly sausage.

> *He bundles* CONRAD *out of the room.*

> GRETA *is left with her mum. It's like they're not sure what to say to each other.*

JANET: Look at you in your blue suit.

> JANET *seems to drift off a little, looking at Greta's room.* GRETA *sees the sadness in her eyes.*

GRETA: Mum? Are you okay?

> JANET *looks at* GRETA. *She doesn't know what to say. It's as if she wants to cry, Like the walls are crumbling around her. She tries to smile bravely.*

JANET: Of course.

> JANET *falls back into herself once more, looking at the room around her.* GRETA *takes her mum's hand in her own, giving it a gentle squeeze.*

CONRAD *calls from downstairs.*

CONRAD: [*off*] *Cake time, people! Where's my girl?!*

GRETA: That's us, Mum. We better go down.

They turn and start to head towards the door.

JANET: This room is such a pigsty. It's like a bomb's hit it.

GRETA: Jeez, alright! Let me at least finish my own party first before I worry about that stuff, Janet.

JANET stops and looks sharply at GRETA.

What?

JANET shakes her head and tuts.

They both walk from the room.

The room sits empty for a few moments.

The objects, like the cranes and the pictures and all the things that have previously come to life, start to glow a little.

The window opens and LITTLE GRETA *climbs in with the music box in her hands.*

She sits cross-legged near the window. She unlocks the box and the music starts to play. She's lost in the music.

After a few moments GRETA *slips quietly into the room. A smile gently breaks across her face.* LITTLE GRETA *looks up at her and smiles, eventually looking back down, getting lost again in the music box.*

The lights slowly fade.

THE END